An Educational

Read and Color

Book of

POISONOUS SNAKES

MW01197026

EDITOR
Linda Spizzirri

COPY REFERENCE
Department of
the Interior

ILLUSTRATION
Peter M. Spizzirri

COVER ART
Peter M. Spizzirri

CONTENTS

This Is An Educational Read and Color Book of POISONOUS SNAKES • Published by SPIZZIRRI PUBLISHING, INC., P.O. BOX 9397, RAPID CITY, SOUTH DAKOTA 57709. No part of this publication may be reproduced, stored in a retrievable system, or transmitted in any form without the express written consent of the publisher. All national and international rights reserved on the entire contents of this publication. Printed in U.S.A.

NAME: WATER MOCCASIN
                         (*Ancistrodon piscivorus*)

WHERE IT IS FOUND: SOUTHEASTERN UNITED STATES

WHERE IT LIVES: AROUND WATER, SWAMPS AND
                         SHALLOW LAKES. LIVES ON LAND
                         BUT HUNTS IN THE WATER

SIZE: UP TO 5 FEET LONG

WHAT IT EATS: DUCKS, FISH, FROGS, MUSKRATS,
                         BIRDS, EGGS, AND OTHER SNAKES

COLOR IT: EITHER OVERALL RAN BODY WITH
                         BROWN BANDS OR DARK OLIVE
                         GREEN BODY AND BLACK BANDS

INTERESTING FACTS:

Because the water moccasin is a pit viper, it has a "pit" or hole between its eye and nostril. This pit is sensitive to the body heat of other animals and enable the snake to find its warm blooded prey. The water moccasin opens its mouth and vibrates its tail as a warning when it is disturbed. Because the lining of its mouth is white, it has been nicknamed the "cotton mouth." Young water moccasins are born alive in broods of 5 to 15.

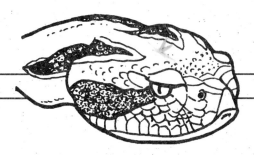

NAME:	DEATH ADDER
	(*Acanthophis antarcticus*)
WHERE IT IS FOUND:	AUSTRALIA
WHERE IT LIVES:	IN ALL PARTS OF THE COUNTRY EXCEPT THE CENTRAL DESERT
SIZE:	3 FEET LONG
WHAT IT EATS:	MOSTLY LIZARDS
COLOR IT:	COLORS WILL VARY DEPENDING ON HABITAT. BASICALLY IT IS DARK GREENISH-BROWN WITH BLACK BODY BANDS. GRAY UNDERBODY

INTERESTING FACTS:

The "death adder" is so named because half of the people who are unlucky enough to be bitten, do in fact, die. Because of its size and shape, it was improperly named as an adder when it was first discovered. The name remains, even though it is not an adder at all, but a member of the cobra family.
This snake often hunts by lying coiled up and wiggling its pointed tail in front of its face to attract lizards.

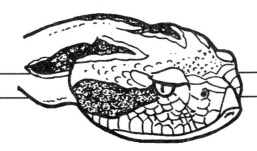

NAME: LONG-NOSED TREE SNAKE
(*Dryophis nasuta*)

WHERE IT'S FOUND: CEYLON, INDIA, MALAYA, AND THE EAST INDIES

WHERE IT LIVES: IN TREES AND BUSHES

SIZE: FEMALE – 6 FEET
MALE – 6 1/2 FEET

WHAT IT EATS: LIZARDS, BIRDS, RODENTS, AND OTHER SNAKES

COLOR IT: YELLOW EYE, NECK, AND LOWER HALF OF FACE. YELLOW STRIPE OVER EYE TO THE TIP OF THE NOSE. OVERALL BRIGHT GREEN; LIGHTER GREEN ON THE BELLY

INTERESTING FACTS:

This long nosed tree snake gives birth to live young in a litter of 3 to 20 snakes. Its long thin body can mover very quickly through bushes and trees. It is a rear fanged snake that holds on to its prey after it strikes, waiting for the venom to do its work. It is not dangerous to man, and actually moves away whenever people come near it.

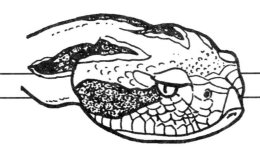

NAME:	EASTERN DIAMONDBACK RATTLE-SNAKE (*Crotalus adamanteus*)
WHERE IT IS FOUND:	Southeastern United States. South from the Carolinas and west to Louisiana
WHERE IT LIVES:	Mainly wooded areas
SIZE:	Averages 5 to 8 feet
WHAT IT EATS:	Rabbits and other mammals, birds
COLOR IT:	Brown body overall. Yellowish gray diamond shapes on body. Black or brown inside the diamond shapes. Black tail, rattle, and face mask.

INTERESTING FACTS:

The Eastern diamondback is the largest poisonous snake found in North America. This snake does not move away to avoid trouble, but rather, will always defend its right to be where it is. It will savagely attack an animal or man that has disturbed its territory. It is a dangerous snake, whose rattle gives no warning until the intruder is very close.

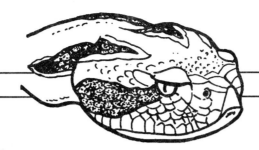

NAME: RUSSELS VIPER (*Vipera russelli*)

WHERE IT IS FOUND: India and southern Asia, plus some East Indian islands

WHERE IT LIVES: In any habitat

SIZE: 5 1/4 feet

WHAT IT EATS: Rodents, frogs, lizards, and birds

COLOR IT: Tan body overall. Red spots that are outlined in black, in rows on its back and sides. White "V" on the head

INTERESTING FACTS:

This snake is more slender than the other vipers, but is one of the most feared snakes of India, Burma, and Siam. When this snake strikes, it injects a large amount of venom into its victim, causing the poison to act quickly. It is made even more dangerous by the fact that the people in these countries go barefoot, thereby increasing the chances of being bitten.
20 to 60 live young are born in each litter.

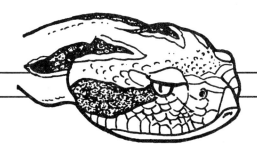

NAME: BLACK MAMBA
                         (*Dendroaspis polylepis*)

WHERE IT IS FOUND: Most of Africa, south of the Sahara
                         Desert

WHERE IT LIVES: Open bush country or among rocks
                         that are close to water

SIZE: Averages 8 or 9 feet. Can be up to 14
                         feet.

WHAT IT EATS: Mainly birds and small mammals such
                         as squirrels

COLOR IT: Dark brown with gray underbody

INTERESTING FACTS:

The black mamba does not have a hood like the cobra does, but it does inflate its neck when it is angry. Being able to move at 7 miles an hour, with bursts of speed up to 15 miles per hour, this snake is the fastest of all snakes. It can accurately strike in any direction, even on the move. It is one of the most aggressive poisonous snakes in the world and is greatly feared by man.

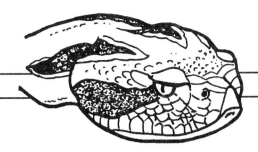

NAME:	KING COBRA (*Ophiophagus hannah*)
WHERE IT IS FOUND:	India, southern China, southern East Asia
WHERE IT LIVES:	Prefers the plains, but also lives in the hills and mountains
SIZE:	14 to 18 1/2 feet
WHAT IT EATS:	All other snakes, harmless or poisonous, including other cobras
COLOR IT:	Dark shades of brown on head and body. Light brown under body.

INTERESTING FACTS:

The king cobra is the longest poisonous snake in the world. This daytime hunter, is the only snake that builds a nest and cares for its young. The female forms an arc with its upper body enabling her to drag decaying sticks and vegetation into a pile to form a nest. After laying and covering her eggs, the female sometimes accompanied by the male, will stand guard and protect the nest until the young are hatched. They protect the nest with such fervor that they will rush out to attack anyone or anything that comes even remotely close to it.

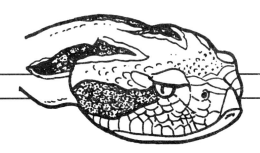

NAME:	COPPERHEAD (*Ancistrodon contortix*)
WHERE IT IS FOUND:	In the U.S. from Massachusetts west to eastern Nebraska. From western Texas east throughout the south; except Florida
WHERE IT LIVES:	Prefers woods and plenty of leafy cover
SIZE:	2 to 4 1/2 feet
WHAT IT EATS:	Small mammals, snakes, lizards and large insects
COLOR IT:	Light reddish tan with dark brown hourglass shaped and spots over entire body. Inside of hourglass shapes are lighter brown

INTERESTING FACTS:

When this snake is angry, it shakes its tail among dead leaves that are on the ground to make itself sound like a rattlesnake. It is not a hostile snake and will actually retire if confronted, but if provoked it can strike swiftly and savagely. In the autumn, it is not uncommon for copperheads to group together with rattlesnakes in a single den to hibernate for the winter.

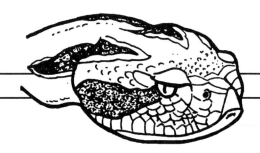

NAME:	BUSHMASTER (*Lachesis muta*)
WHERE IT IS FOUND:	Northern South America, Costa Rica, and Panama
WHERE IT LIVES:	Forests
SIZE:	Up to 12 feet in length
WHAT IT EATS:	Mainly small mammals
COLOR IT:	Overall gray body with light gray underbody. Dark brown spine and diamond shaped spots and patterns on entire body

INTERESTING FACTS:

The bushmaster is the longest of the pit viper snakes in Central and South America. Because of its long body, it can strike from a great distance. This makes it one of the most dangerous American snakes. It also has large venom glands and very long fangs. A 6 foot bushmaster can have fangs that are an inch or more long. The female is believed to stand guard over her nest, which has approximately 12 eggs.

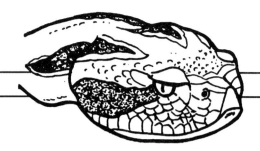

NAME:	SIDEWINDER (Crotalus cerastes)
WHERE IT IS FOUND:	Southwestern United States
WHERE IT LIVES:	Loose desert sands
SIZE:	1 1/2 to 2 1/2 feet. The female is larger than the male
WHAT IT EATS:	Rodents, lizards, birds, other snakes, even other sidewinders
COLOR IT:	Overall light tan-gray with brown spots. Large brown wing shapes the length of its spine with smaller white arrow shapes between them

INTERESTING FACTS:

The sidewinder gets its name from the unusual looping side movement it uses to move quickly over the loose desert sand. It is sometimes called the "horned rattlesnake" because it has a large scale, like a horn, above each eye. During the day it buries itself in the sand and hunts in the early part of the night when its prey is most active.

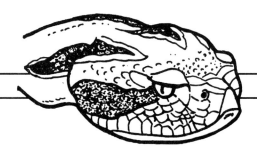

NAME:	BLACK AND YELLOW SEA SNAKE (*Pelamis platurus*)
WHERE IT IS FOUND:	Off coasts of Asia, Persian Gulf, Japan, and Australia
WHERE IT LIVES:	Only in the water
SIZE:	3 1/2 feet
WHAT IT EATS:	Eel and fish
COLOR IT:	Yellow body and lower jaw. Top of head is black. Black spine stripe and black spotted tail

INTERESTING FACTS:

Its flattened body and tail enable this snake to be a fast swimmer that is more at home in the sea than any other sea snake. It does not venture onto land in its entire life. It mates and gives birth to live young while remaining in the ocean. It can sometimes be found hundreds of miles from land and has even been known to cross the entire Pacific Ocean.

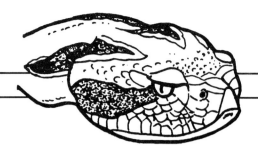

NAME:	EASTERN CORAL SNAKE (*Micrurus fulvius*)
WHERE IT IS FOUND:	Southeastern United States west to Texas
WHERE IT LIVES:	Grasslands and open woods
SIZE:	Averages 20 to 30 inches
WHAT IT EATS:	Snakes and lizards
COLOR IT:	Snout and every other band is black (shaded on art). Narrow band is yellow. Red bands have black spots

INTERESTING FACTS:

The Eastern coral snake is a close relative of the cobra. It is rarely seen because it hides and rests during the day and comes out to hunt at night. This snake lays its eggs under a log or in a hollowed spot in the earth. 10 or 12 weeks later, 7 inch long young are born. They are pale in color and as they grow older their colors get brighter.

The Eastern coral snake has short fangs and chews the bite area of its victim to give many doses of venom, thereby killing its prey. It rarely bites humans, and will strike only if stepped on or handled.

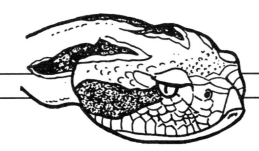

NAME:	RHINOCEROS VIPER (*Bitis nasicornis*)
WHERE IT IS FOUND:	Africa
WHERE IT LIVES:	In tropical forests
SIZE:	Up to 4 feet long
WHAT IT EATS:	Small ground birds and frogs, mammals, toads and lizards
COLOR IT:	Tan over all. Shaded areas are black. Light blue butterfly shapes with thin yellow outlines on spine. Reddish brown triangle shapes on sides of body and between butterfly shapes

INTERESTING FACTS:

This snake got its name from the two large upright scales at the end of its snout. It is a very mild mannered snake that must be forced into defending itself. Its bright colors blend in perfectly with the surroundings in its native forests. The dead leaves, green leaves, and grass make it almost impossible to see unless it is moving.

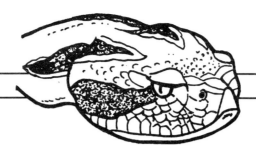

NAME:	EUROPEAN VIPER (*Vipera berus*)
WHERE IS IT FOUND:	England, Scotland, Scandinavia, all of Europe, Asia to China and eastern Russia
WHERE IT LIVES:	Any kind of habitat
SIZE:	Female – 25 1/2 inches Male – 28 1/2 inches
WHAT IT EATS:	Voles, lizards, or anything it can swallow
COLOR IT:	Greenish-brown with black zigzag lines down entire length of its back. Black spots on side of its body. Head has a black "V" or "X" on the top

INTERESTING FACTS:

The European viper is one of the most wide ranging of all snakes. It is mainly active during the day. It does not have ears to hear but rather puts its jaw to the ground to feel the vibrations. This is how it can tell what is around it and where its prey might be.

In March, the European viper emerges from its winter sleep and in April it starts looking for a mate. It is common for 2 or 3 males to compete for a single female. In the fighting ritual the snakes do not bite one another. Rather, the fight is over when one snake succeeds in pressing the loser to the ground. In early September, from six to twelve living young are born.

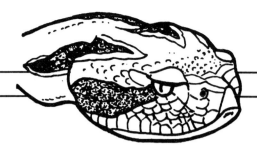

NAME:	FER DE LANCE (*Bothrops atrox*)
WHERE IT IS FOUND:	Northern Mexico to Argentina. West Indies islands of Martinique, Tobago, Santa Lucia, and Trinidad
WHERE IT LIVES:	Adaptable to most habitats. Even lives near man to hunt rats and mice
SIZE:	Averages 4 to 5 feet, but can grow to 8 feet
WHAT IT EATS:	Rodents, frogs, lizards, small snakes and opossums
COLOR IT:	Brownish gray overall. Light gray diamond shapes and spots on entire body. Black or dark brown inside diamond shapes or spots

INTERESTING FACTS:

This fearless snake has a habit of coming out at night and lying on roads and foot paths where people walk. It does not fear man at all, and strikes if it is disturbed. The Fer de Lance has long sharp fangs and strong venom. This snake causes several thousand deaths a year in Central and South America.

The young are born alive and venomous in litters of 60 to 80 or more.

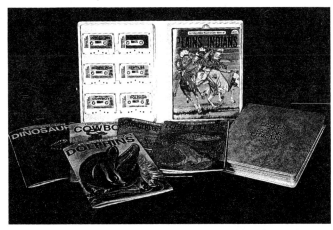